THE KINGS OF WEALTH
9 Habits Of Successful People.

Reign Godall

All rights reserved. No part of this publication may be reproduced, distributed, or transmitted in any form or by any means, including photocopying, recording, or other electronic or mechanical methods, without the prior written permission of the publisher, except in the case of brief quotations embodied in critical reviews and certain other noncommercial uses permitted by copyright law.

Copyright © Reign Godall, 2022.

Table of Contents.

JEFF BEZOS

MARK ZUCKERBERG

BILL GATES

ELON MUSK

9 HABITS OF HIGHLY EFFECTIVE AND SUCCESSFUL PEOPLE.

8 THINGS TO TAKE AWAY FROM THESE MEN

JEFF BEZOS

Jeff Bezos, full name Jeffrey Preston Bezos, was the founder and CEO of Amazon.com, Inc., an online retailer of books and subsequently of a broad range of commodities. On January 12, 1964, he was born in Albuquerque, New Mexico. Under his leadership, Amazon grew to become the world's biggest online retailer and the gold standard for online commerce.

Career and young adulthood

While still in high school, Bezos established the Dream Institute, a place that encouraged young people to think imaginatively. He worked in a number of fields before joining the New York financial firm D.E. Shaw graduated from Princeton University in 1986 with degrees in electrical engineering and computer science. Shaw & Co. was founded in 1990. Bezos, the company's youngest senior vice president, was tasked with investigating the financial opportunities provided by the Internet. His business imagination was sparked by its enormous potential—Web use was growing at a rate of more than 2,000% each year. He left D.E. in 1994. Shaw and his business partner relocated to Seattle, Washington, to create an online bookshop. Bezos started developing the site's software while working from his garage with a small team. Amazon, named after a South American river, sold its first book in July 1995.

Personal Existence

After meeting Mackenzie Tuttle at D.E., Bezos married her in 1993. Shaw. When the couple divorced in January 2019, the National Enquirer released a report the next day revealing that Bezos was having an affair with another lady. Bezos then started looking into how the tabloid acquired access to his personal text messages. Then, in February, he published a lengthier post online in which he accused American Media Inc. (AMI), the Enquirer's owner, of "extortion and bribery" for allegedly threatening to publish nude photographs of Bezos if he did not drop his investigation and making other demands. According to the Bezos-led investigation, his lover's brother later revealed the messages.

Amazon.com

Amazon quickly rose to the top of the e-commerce industry. The service, which was open 24 hours a day, encouraged users to post their own book reviews and provided discounts, personalized book suggestions, and searches for out-of-print titles. In June 1998, it began selling CDs, and later that year, it began selling DVDs. In 1999, Bezos invested in new online firms and added auctions to the website. Amazon's success inspired other companies, including well-known book retailers, to open online storefronts.

As additional companies competed for Internet money, Bezos saw the need for diversification, and by 2005, Amazon was providing a wide range of products, including consumer electronics, clothing, and hardware. Introducing Amazon Web Services (AWS), a cloud computing business that grew to become the world's biggest of its kind, allowing Amazon to diversify even more in 2006. Amazon introduced the Kindle, a digital book reader with wireless Internet access, in late 2007. It allows customers to buy, download, read, and save a huge variety of books on demand. Amazon announced in 2010 that Kindle book sales have surpassed hardcover book sales. Amazon began producing its own television episodes and feature films with the launch of its Amazon Studios division. Amazon's annual net sales increased from $510,000 in 1995 to over $600 million in 1998, and from more than $19.1 billion in 2008 to almost $233 billion in 2018. In 2018, AWS accounted for about half of the company's operational earnings. Amazon earned record earnings two years later, and its fourth-quarter sales surpassed $100 billion for the first time. The COVID-19 epidemic increased property purchases, which contributed to the record high figures.

Bezos announced in February 2021 that he will step down as CEO at the end of the year.

He did, however, intend to remain as executive chairman of Amazon.

In addition to Amazon, Bezos founded Blue Origin, a spaceflight company, in 2000. Blue Origin soon after purchased a launch site in Texas with plans to launch an orbital launch vehicle, New Glenn, in 2020 and a crewed suborbital spacecraft, New Shepard, in 2018. In 2013, Bezos paid $250 million for The Washington Post and its sibling businesses. Bezos is the world's wealthiest individual, with a net worth of $112 billion in 2018.

MARK ZUCKERBERG

Mark Zuckerberg: Who Is He?

The social networking site Facebook was co-founded by Mark Zuckerberg when he was still a student at Harvard University. After his second year of college, Zuckerberg dropped out to concentrate on the website, whose user base has now expanded to over two billion, making Zuckerberg a multi-millionaire. The 2010 movie The

Social Network included a representation of Facebook's beginnings.

Early Years

Zuckerberg was born on May 14, 1984, into a wealthy, highly educated family in White Plains, New York. He was raised in the neighboring town of Dobbs Ferry.

Edward Zuckerberg, the father of Mark Zuckerberg, had a dental practice next door to the family home. Prior to the birth of the couple's four children—Mark, Randi, Donna, and Arielle—his mother, Karen, worked as a psychiatrist.

Early on, Zuckerberg had an interest in computers. Around the age of 12, he used Atari BASIC to create a messaging program he called "Zucknet." In order to notify him of a new patient without shouting across the room, his father utilized the application in his dentist's practice. Zucknet was also used by the family to communicate inside the house.

He also created computer games with his friends just for fun. He said, "I had a lot of friends who were artists. They would visit, draw something, and I would create a game from it.

Education of Mark Zuckerberg

Zuckerberg's parents hired private computer trainer David Newman to visit the house once a week and work with Zuckerberg in order to keep up with Zuckerberg's growing interest in computers. Later, Newman told reporters that it was challenging to keep up with the prodigy, who began enrolling in graduate courses at nearby Mercy College about this time.

Following that, Zuckerberg enrolled at the pricey prep school Phillips Exeter Academy in New Hampshire. He showed off his fencing prowess there and was named team captain for the school. He earned a diploma in classics for his literary accomplishments as well.

Zuckerberg, though, remained enthralled by computers and persisted in focusing on developing new apps. He created Synapse, an early version of Pandora's music service, when he was still a high school student.

AOL and Microsoft were among the businesses who indicated interest in buying the program and hiring the student before graduation. He declined the proposals.

Experiences in College for Mark Zuckerberg
Zuckerberg enrolled at Harvard University in 2002 after receiving his diploma from Exeter. After his second year of college,

Zuckerberg quit to focus entirely on his new company, Facebook.

He had established himself as the go-to software developer on campus by the time he was in his second year at the Ivy League institution. He created the CourseMatch service at that time, which allowed students to choose their courses based on the preferences of other users.

He also introduced Facemash, a website that allowed users to vote on which of two students' photos from the same university they thought was more attractive. The school administration finally decided that the program was inappropriate and shut it down, despite the fact that it had become very popular.

Three of his classmates—Divya Narendra, Cameron, and Tyler Winklevoss—asked him to assist with them on a proposal for a social networking site they called Harvard

Connection because of the excitement around his earlier attempts. This website was developed to serve as a dating service for the Harvard elite by using data from the student networks at Harvard.

Despite having agreed to help with the project, Zuckerberg swiftly left to develop on his own social networking platform, The Facebook.

Mark Zuckerberg founded Facebook.

The Facebook was a website that allowed users to create their own profiles, upload photographs, and communicate with other people when it was first created by Mark Zuckerberg, Dustin Moskovitz, Chris Hughes, and Eduardo Saverin. Up until June 2004, the team ran the website from a dorm room at Harvard University.

Zuckerberg moved the business to Palo Alto, California, that year while forgoing his college education. One million people were using Facebook as of the year 2004.

Zuckerberg's group received a significant boost from Accel Partners, a venture capital firm, in 2005. The network, which at the time was only accessible to Ivy League students, cost Accel $12.7 million.

By granting access to more institutions, high schools, and foreign schools, Zuckerberg's company increased the site's user base to more than 5.5 million by December 2005. Other businesses began to take notice of the website as they sought to promote on the well-known social hub.

Zuckerberg turned down approaches from companies like Yahoo! and MTV Networks because he didn't want to sell out. Instead, he concentrated on building up the website, inviting additional developers to work on it, and adding new features.

"Harvard Connection" and Obstacles in the Law

Zuckerberg seemed to be going only up. But in 2006, the business tycoon faced his first significant obstacle: the creators of Harvard Connection claimed that Zuckerberg had stolen their idea and demanded compensation for his financial losses.

According to Zuckerberg, the ideas were based on two quite different categories of social networks. After lawyers analyzed Zuckerberg's archives, incriminating instant messages revealed that Zuckerberg could have intentionally stolen Harvard Connection's intellectual property and distributed the private information of Facebook users to his friends. Then, Zuckerberg expressed sorrow for the damaging texts and apologized. In an interview with The New Yorker, he said, "If you're going to develop a service that is substantial and that a lot of people rely on, then you ought to be mature, right?" "I think I've grown and learned a lot,"

Although the parties reached an early settlement of $65 million, the legal dispute over the matter continued far into 2011 since Narendra and the Winklevosses believed they were misled about the value of their shares.

The film-The Social Network

The Social Network, a film written and directed by Aaron Sorkin, was released in 2010. Eight Academy Award nominations were given to the well acclaimed film.

Ben Mezrich's 2009 book The Accidental Billionaires served as the inspiration for Sorkin's screenplay. Mezrich faced intense criticism for his retelling of Zuckerberg's story, which included made-up details, imaginative language, and fictional characters.

Angrily objecting to the movie's plot, Zuckerberg later told a journalist at The New Yorker that many of the details were untrue. For instance, Zuckerberg had been seeing his girlfriend continuously since 2003. Additionally, he admitted that he had no interest in joining any of the final teams.

At a startup conference in 2010, Zuckerberg told a reporter, "It's fascinating what things they emphasized on getting right; like, every single clothing and fleece that I wore in the movie is truly a shirt or fleece that I own." "So there's all this stuff they got wrong and a bunch of random stuff they got right," one person said.

Despite the criticism, Zuckerberg and Facebook kept on succeeding. In 2010, Vanity Fair named him the top New Establishment, and Time magazine named him Person of the Year.

Facebook IPO

Facebook's first public offering, which it carried out in May 2012 and raised $16 billion from, was the biggest Internet IPO in history.

The price of Facebook shares initially declined after the IPO's initial success, but Zuckerberg is predicted to weather any ups and downs in the market performance of his business.

With Facebook's debut on the Fortune 500 list in 2013, Zuckerberg, then 28 years old, was the list's youngest CEO.

Saga of Cambridge Analytica

Prior to the 2016 U.S. presidential election, Zuckerberg came under fire for the rise of false news stories on his site. He assigned himself the personal goal of developing fresh defenses against nation-state exploitation and manipulation of Facebook users at the beginning of 2018. (Previous personal challenges began on January 1, 2009, and have included learning Mandarin and only eating meat he killed himself.)

He said on his Facebook page, "We won't avoid all mistakes or abuse, but we currently make too many mistakes maintaining our rules and avoiding exploitation of our resources. "If this year goes well, we'll finish 2018 on a significantly better trajectory,"

A few months later, it was discovered that Cambridge Analytica, a data company connected to President Donald Trump's 2016 campaign, had utilized private data from some 87 million Facebook accounts without informing the owners. This brought Zuckerberg under criticism once again. As a consequence of the uproar, investors' faith in Facebook seemed to be shaken; once the news was made public, its shares fell by 15%.

After a few days of radio quiet, Zuckerberg appeared on many platforms to discuss how the firm was taking efforts to restrict the access of third-party developers to user information and declared his willingness to go before Congress.

On Sunday, March 25, Facebook published full-page advertisements in seven British and three American newspapers that were written in Mark Zuckerberg's own words. He promised that the company will review all of its apps and notify customers which ones they might turn off. He wrote, "I'm sorry we didn't do more at the time. "I promise to work harder for you,"

Prior to his two-day hearing on April 10 and 11, Zuckerberg visited Capitol Hill and talked with senators amid growing calls for his resignation from investor groups. The Senate Commerce and Judiciary Committees' first day of hearings was seen as a pleasant event, with numerous senators clearly attempting to understand the business strategy that supported the social media behemoth.

After the first hearing, the House Energy and Commerce Committee's members interrogated the Facebook CEO on privacy issues, which made the exchange more tense. In the course of the day's evidence, Zuckerberg disclosed that Cambridge Analytica had collected his personal data among other data, and he said that governmental regulation of Facebook and other social media firms was "inevitable."

Individual Wealth

The company's growth seemed to be unaffected by the bad publicity surrounding the 2016 election and the Cambridge Analytica controversy, as Facebook's stock closed at a record $203.23 on July 6, 2018. After fellow tech giants Jeff Bezos and Bill Gates, the rise moved Zuckerberg ahead of

Berkshire Hathaway CEO Warren Buffett to claim third place in terms of wealth in the world.

Any gains were lost on July 26 when Facebook shares plunged a startling 19 percent as a result of an earnings report that showed a failure to achieve revenue estimates and a deceleration in user growth. In a single day, about $16 billion of Zuckerberg's personal wealth vanished.

Zuckerberg is still among the richest persons in the world despite the stock's recovery. In 2019, Forbes rated Zuckerberg at No. 8 on their list of "Billionaires," placing him ahead of Google co-founders Larry Page and Sergey Brin (Nos. 10 and 10 respectively) and Microsoft founder Bill Gates (No (No. 14). At the time, the magazine estimated his net worth at around $62.3 billion.

Libra

Facebook said in June 2019 that it will enter the cryptocurrency market with the launch of Libra in 2020. In addition to creating the blockchain technology that will power its financial infrastructure, Facebook founded the Libra Association, a Switzerland-based governing body made up of internet behemoths like Spotify and venture capital companies like Andreessen Horowitz.

As a result of the report, Congress once again targeted Zuckerberg, calling the CEO to appear before the House Financial Service Committee in October. Despite giving guarantees that Facebook would leave the Libra Association if the initiative was rejected by authorities, Zuckerberg was grilled by sceptical MPs who brought up the Cambridge Analytica scandal and other wrongdoings.

Marriage

In 2012, Zuckerberg wed Priscilla Chan, a Chinese-American medical student he had met at Harvard. One day after Facebook's IPO, the long-term pair got married.

The ceremony was held in the couple's Palo Alto, California home in front of around 100 guests. The visitors believed they had come to celebrate Chan's medical school graduation, but they really saw Chan and Zuckerberg exchange vows.
Max was born on November 30, 2015, and August was born on August 28, 2017. Zuckerberg has two children.

The couple posted on Facebook that they were expecting twins. When Max was born, Zuckerberg made the announcement that he would take a two-month paternity leave to be with his family.

Donations and Philanthropic Causes of Mark Zuckerberg

Since accumulating substantial wealth, Zuckerberg has donated millions to a number of charitable organisations. The most famous instances were in September 2010, when he gave $100 million to Newark Public Schools in New Jersey, who were in financial trouble.

Then, in December 2010, Zuckerberg committed to giving at least half of his fortune to charity over his lifetime by signing the "Giving Pledge." Warren Buffett, George Lucas, and Bill Gates are other Giving Pledge participants. Following his gift, Zuckerberg urged other young, successful entrepreneurs to do the same.

There is a great potential for many of us to give back early in our career and witness the effect of our charitable activities, he added, as a generation of younger people who have prospered on the success of their businesses.

In an open letter to their daughter in November 2015, Zuckerberg and his wife also promised to donate 99 percent of their Facebook stock to charity.

The pair stated their commitment in the open letter that was published on Zuckerberg's Facebook page: "We are dedicated to doing our modest bit to help build this future for all children." "During our lifetimes, we will donate 99% of our Facebook shares, which are presently worth roughly $45 billion, to join many others in enhancing our planet for future generations."

To help "cure, prevent, and manage all diseases in our children's lifetime," Zuckerberg and Chan announced in September 2016 that the Chan Zuckerberg Initiative (CZI), the business into which they invested their Facebook shares, would invest at least $3 billion in scientific research over the following ten years. The

Rockefeller University's renowned neuroscientist Cori Bargmann has been appointed CZI's president of science.

A San Francisco-based independent research facility called Chan Zuckerberg Biohub, which will bring together engineers, computer scientists, biologists, chemists, and other members of the scientific community, was also revealed. The first financing for Biohub, a collaboration between Stanford University, the University of California, San Francisco, and the University of California, Berkeley, will be $600 million over 10 years.

BILL GATES

Bill Gates: Who Is He?

Bill Gates, an entrepreneur and businessman, and Paul Allen, a business partner, developed and grew Microsoft, the biggest software company in the world, using cutting-edge technology, astute commercial strategy, and aggressive business practices. Gates grew to be one of the wealthiest men in the world as a result. Gates stated in February 2014 that he was resigning as chairman of Microsoft to concentrate on charity endeavors at his foundation, the Bill and Melinda Gates Foundation.

Early Years

Gates was born in Seattle, Washington, on October 28, 1955, as William Henry Gates III. Gates, his elder sister Kristianne, and his younger sister Libby all grew raised in an upper middle class home. When he first met Mary Maxwell, their future wife, William H. Gates Sr. was a bright but reserved law student. She was a University of Washington student who was engaged in leadership and student affairs and was athletic and personable.

All three of the Gates children were taught to be competitive and strive for greatness in a friendly and close-knit environment. When he organized sporting events for the family at their summer home on Puget Sound, Gates displayed his competitive nature at a young age. He also enjoyed playing board games, with Risk being his favorite, and was a master at the game of Monopoly. Gates and his mother, Mary, who spent her time raising the family, working on charitable causes, and raising the children after a short stint as a teacher, had a very close connection. She has served on a number of business boards, including those of International Business Machines, the United Way, and Seattle's First Interstate Bank, which was established by her family (IBM). When she helped in schools and in community groups, she often brought Gates with her.

Education

As a youngster, Gates devoured books and would spend countless hours reading over reference materials like encyclopedias. When Gates was approximately 11 or 12, his parents started to worry about his conduct. Although he was performing well in school, his parents were concerned that he would end up becoming a loner since he sometimes appeared bored and disengaged.

Although they were ardent supporters of free public education, Gates' parents put him at Seattle's elite preparatory Lakeside School when he became 13 years old. He excelled in almost every topic, particularly math and physics, while also performing quite well in theater and English.

A Seattle-based computer business provided the pupils computer time while they were at Lakeside School. The Mother's Club bought a teletype terminal for the pupils to use using money from the school's rummage sale. Gates was fascinated by what a computer was capable of, and he devoted a lot of his leisure time to working on the terminal. He created a BASIC computer software in which users may play tic tac toe against the machine.

Gates received his Lakeside diploma in 1973. He achieved a feat of intellectual prowess by scoring 1590 out of 1600 on the college SAT exam, which he spoke about for many years while meeting new people.

In the autumn of 1973, Gates enrolled at Harvard University with the intention of pursuing a legal career. Gates walked out of college in 1975 to start his firm, Microsoft, much to the dismay of his parents.

In contrast to attending classes, Gates spent more time in the computer lab. He didn't exactly follow a study schedule; he managed to pass the exam with a passable mark while just getting a few hours of sleep and cramming for a test.

Joining Forces With Paul Allen

At Lakeside School, Gates had the opportunity to meet Allen, who was two years his senior. Despite being quite different individuals, the two quickly become close friends. They shared a love of technology. Allen was more quiet and reserved. Gates was tenacious and sometimes aggressive.

Despite their disagreements, Allen and Gates collaborated often on initiatives in their spare time. Sometimes the two would argue over who was correct or who ought to operate the computer lab. When their dispute got out of hand, Allen once forbade Gates from using the computer lab.

At one point, Gates and Allen's access to the school's computers was terminated because they had been abusing software flaws to get free computer time from the computer provider. When they promised to help with software debugging after their probation, they were given access to the computer lab once again. Gates created a scheduling software for the school and a payroll program for the computer firm the guys had broken into at this period.

At the age of 15, Gates and Allen founded their own company and created "Traf-o-Data," a computer software that tracked Seattle's traffic patterns. They made $20,000 as a result of their work. Gates' parents wanted him to graduate from high school and go on to college, where they thought he would pursue a career as a lawyer. Despite this, Gates and Allen decided to create their own business.

Gates attended Harvard University while Allen attended Washington State University, but the two remained in contact. Allen left college after two years and relocated to Boston, Massachusetts, where he started working for Honeywell. He then displayed a copy of Popular Electronics magazine to Gates, which had an article on the Altair 8800 minicomputer kit. The potential of what this machine may provide in the field of personal computing captivated both young guys.

Micro Instrumentation and Telemetry Systems, a tiny business in Albuquerque, New Mexico, produced the Altair (MITS). Gates and Allen got in touch with the business and said they were developing BASIC software that would operate the Altair computer. They really lacked an Altair and the programming necessary to operate it, but they nevertheless wanted to know whether MITS was interested in hiring someone to create such software.

Ed Roberts, the president of MITS, invited the lads to do a demonstration. Gates and Allen hurriedly wrote the BASIC program in Harvard's computer lab over the course of the next two months. Allen had never tested it out on an Altair computer, so he made the trip to Albuquerque for a test run at MITS. It performed flawlessly. Gates left Harvard shortly after Allen was given a job at MITS and joined him there. They established Microsoft together.

Allen stayed at Microsoft up until 1983, when he received a Hodgkin's disease diagnosis. Allen left the firm even though his cancer was in remission a year later after receiving aggressive therapy. As to why Allen quit Microsoft, there are several rumors. Some claim that Gates kicked him out, but many claim that Allen had a life-changing event and realized there were other things he could devote his attention to.

Microsoft

Gates and Allen established Microsoft in 1975 as a combination of "microcomputer" and "software" (they dropped the hyphen within a year). The first item produced by the business was BASIC software for the Altair computer.

It wasn't all plain sailing at first. Microsoft's BASIC software for the Altair computer brought in a charge and royalties for the corporation, but it wasn't enough to cover costs. In subsequent years, Gates claimed that only 10% of those utilizing BASIC on the Altair computer had really paid for it.

Computer enthusiasts were big fans of Microsoft's BASIC program; they got pre-market versions and shared them for free. Many aficionados of personal computers at the time didn't do it for the money. They believed that since software was so easily reproduced and distributed, people might share it with friends and other computer aficionados. Gates had a different viewpoint. Especially when it included software that was designed to be sold, he considered the free distribution of software to be theft.

Gates warned computer enthusiasts in an open letter he published in February 1976 that continuing to share and use software without paying for it would "prevent new software from being produced." In essence, software piracy would deter developers from devoting time and resources to producing high-quality software. Computer aficionados disliked the letter, but Gates adhered to his convictions and often used the danger of innovation as a defense against accusations of unethical corporate tactics.

Ed Roberts, the president of MITS, and Gates had a contentious relationship that often degenerated into altercations. Roberts and the combative Gates disagreed on the direction of the company and the development of software. Roberts thought Gates was rude and spoiled.

Roberts sold MITS to a different computer business in 1977 and then returned to Georgia to enroll in medical school and pursue a career as a doctor.

Allen and Gates were left alone. To save the software rights they had created for Altair, the couple had to file a lawsuit against the new owner of MITS. Beginning in 1979, Gates relocated Microsoft's offices to Bellevue, Washington, which is located just east of Seattle. Microsoft produced software in a variety of forms for other computer firms.

Gates poured himself into his job, happy to be back in the Pacific Northwest. The new company's 25 workers were given extensive duties for all elements of the firm, including marketing, business growth, and product development.

Although the business had a rocky beginning, by 1979 Microsoft was making around $2.5 million. Gates positioned himself as the company's leader at the age of 23. He oversaw operations and served as the organization's spokesman with his expertise in software development and great business sense. Every line of code the business released was carefully examined by Gates, who often rewrote code himself when he deemed it essential.

Software from Microsoft for IBM PCs

Gates was constantly traveling and praising Microsoft software programs while the computer industry expanded and firms like Apple, Intel, and IBM created hardware and components. He often brought his mother along. Mary served on various business boards, including IBM's, and was well-known and well regarded. Gates first connected with the CEO of IBM via Mary.

In November 1980, IBM contacted Microsoft in search of software to run its impending personal computer (PC). According to legend, someone at IBM requested Gates to serve coffee at their first meeting since they believed him to be an office assistant.

42

Despite his youthful appearance, Gates rapidly won over IBM, persuading them that he and his business could satisfy their demands. The main issue was that IBM's new machines would not be able to run Microsoft's foundational operating system.

Not to be deterred, Gates purchased an operating system designed to operate on machines comparable to IBM's PC. He struck an agreement with the creator of the program, making Microsoft the exclusive agent for licensing and subsequently the sole owner of the property, while keeping IBM in the dark about the arrangement.

Later, when Gates and Microsoft withheld crucial information, the business filed a lawsuit. Microsoft reached an out-of-court settlement for an undisclosed sum without making any admissions of guilt on the part of Gates or Microsoft.

Gates had to modify the recently acquired software so that it would run on the IBM PC. He charged $50,000 to deliver it, the same amount he had paid to purchase the software initially. IBM sought to acquire the operating system's source code, which would have given them access to it. Instead of agreeing, Gates suggested that IBM pay a license fee for copies of the software that was sold with their machines. By doing this, Microsoft was able to license the MS-DOS operating system to any other PC maker in the event that other tech firms decided to copy the IBM PC, which they soon did. Microsoft furthermore made available a program called Softcard that made it possible for Apple II computers to run Microsoft BASIC.

Microsoft's business expanded between 1979 and 1981 with the creation of software for IBM. Revenue soared from $2.5 million to $16 million as staff grew from 25 to 128. Midway through 1981, Gates and Allen incorporated Microsoft, and Gates was named CEO and board chairman. As executive vice president, Allen was appointed.

In 1983, Microsoft opened operations in Japan and Great Britain as part of its worldwide expansion. Its software was used by 30 percent of PCs worldwide.

Competition With Steve Jobs

Microsoft and Apple shared many of their early inventions even though their rivalry is legendary. When Steve Jobs was still the company's CEO in 1981, Apple approached Microsoft to assist in creating software for Macintosh computers. Both the creation of Microsoft and the creation of Microsoft programs for Macintosh included several developers. Some of the common names between the Microsoft and Macintosh platforms were evidence of the partnership. Through the exchange of information,

Microsoft was able to create Windows, a system that displayed text and pictures on the screen using a mouse to control a graphical user interface. This was quite different from the MS-DOS text-and-keyboard system, where all text formatting appeared on the screen as code rather than what would be printed.

Gates was quick to understand the danger that such software would represent to MS-DOS and the whole Microsoft organization. The rival VisiCorp software running on a Macintosh machine would be so much simpler to use for the less tech-savvy user—which was the majority of the purchasing public.

A new Microsoft operating system with a graphical user interface was in the works, Gates said in an ad campaign. It would go by the name "Windows" and work with all PC applications created for the MS-DOS operating system. The statement was a bluff since Microsoft didn't have a similar product in the works. It was a brilliant marketing strategy. The MS-DOS operating system was used by over 30% of computer users, who preferred to wait for Windows software than switching to a new platform. By early 1985, the VisiCorp system had lost its impetus since no one was ready to create applications in a different format for it.

Nearly two years after making his statement, Gates and Microsoft introduced Windows in November 1985. Visually, the Windows operating system resembled the Macintosh operating system that Apple Computer Corporation had released over two years previously.

In the past, when Microsoft was attempting to make its products compatible with Apple computers, Apple had previously granted Microsoft complete access to their technologies. Apple refused Gates' recommendation to license their software because they were more interested in making money from the sale of computers.

Once again, Gates made the most of the circumstance by developing software that was eerily identical to the Macintosh. Microsoft replied by threatening to postpone the delivery of its Microsoft-compatible software for Macintosh customers when Apple threatened legal action.

Microsoft ultimately won the legal battle. It may demonstrate that while the two software systems performed similarly, each specific function was quite different.

A Good Name in the Industry

Despite Microsoft's prosperity, Gates never really felt safe. Gates acquired a fierce desire and competitive spirit by always looking over his shoulder to see how the rival was doing. When Gates' assistant arrived at work early, she saw someone dozing off beneath a desk. Before realizing it was Gates, she thought of contacting security or the police.

Because of his brilliance, Gates was able to understand the software business from all angles, including corporate strategy and product development. He created a profile of all the potential scenarios and ran through them, asking questions about everything that may happen, while examining any company decision.

He expected the same level of commitment from everyone in the organization. His combative management style, which included challenging staff members and their ideas to spur on the creative process, became legendary. Gates may be heard saying, "That's the craziest thing I've ever heard!" to an unprepared presentation.

Both Gates' love for his business and the employee's rigor were put to the test in this situation. He was always assessing whether others around him were really persuaded by their views.

Leaving Microsoft

Steve Ballmer, a buddy from college who had worked for Microsoft since 1980, was appointed CEO after Gates stepped aside from day-to-day management of the company in 2000. Although he continued to serve as chairman of the board, Gates positioned himself as chief software architect to focus on the area of the company that was more personally meaningful to him.

Gates said in 2006 that he was leaving Microsoft's full-time workforce in order to spend more time at the foundation. He left Microsoft on June 27, 2008, for the last time.

Gates resigned as Microsoft's chairman in February 2014 to take on a new role as a technical consultant. Satya Nadella, 46, took over as CEO of Microsoft in lieu of longtime leader Steve Ballmer.

Personal Life

Melinda French, a 23-year-old Microsoft product manager, drew Bill Gates' attention when he was 32 years old in 1987. Gates was an ideal fit for the very intelligent and well-organized Melinda. Their bond strengthened over time as they realized they had a close-knit mind. Melinda and Gates wed in Hawaii on January 1st, 1994.

They took a break in 1995 to travel and get a fresh perspective on life and the world following the tragic loss of his mother to breast cancer only a few months after their wedding. Jennifer, their first child, was born in 1996. Their second daughter, Phoebe, was born in 2002, and their boy, Rory, was born in 1999.

In May 2021, the couple gave notice that their marriage was ending.

Wealth

At the age of 31, Gates became a billionaire overnight when he took Microsoft public in March 1986 with an IPO at $21 per share. At the time, Gates owned $234 million of Microsoft's $520 million in shares, or 45 percent of the company's 24.7 million shares.

The value of the company's shares grew throughout time and it was divided multiple times. Upon the stock's reaching a share price of $90.75 in 1987, Gates became a billionaire. Since that time, Gates has consistently been at the top of Forbes' yearly list of the 400 richest Americans, if not at the top. When stock prices reached an all-time high in 1999 and the stock had increased eightfold since its first public offering, Gates' net worth momentarily exceeded $101 billion.

Gates and his family relocated into a 55,000 square foot home on Lake Washington's coast in 1997. Even though the home doubles as a business hub, the couple and their three kids are claimed to find it to be extremely comfortable.

The Foundation of Bill and Melinda Gates

The William H. Gates Foundation was founded by Bill and Melinda in 1994 with the intention of advancing global health, education, and low-income communities. The group also deals with domestic concerns, such assisting American kids in becoming college-ready.

Bill had developed an interest in becoming a civic leader in the mold of his mother thanks to Melinda, who encouraged him to research the charitable endeavors of American industrial giants Andrew Carnegie and John D. Rockefeller. He came to the conclusion that he owed it to charity to donate more of his fortune.

In order to create the Bill & Melinda Gates Foundation in 2000, the couple consolidated multiple family charities and contributed $28 billion. Bill's work with the Bill & Melinda Gates Foundation took up a lot of his time and energy during the next several years.

Gates has focused most of his time and effort on the activities of the Bill & Melinda Gates Foundation since leaving Microsoft. Gates advocated for charter schools and the Common Core national standards for grades K through 12 in 2015. When the foundation announced that it will provide its workers with a year of paid leave after the birth or adoption of a child around this time, Gates further demonstrated his status as a trailblazing employer.

The first of the foundation's yearly "Goalkeepers" reports, which examines advancements in a number of significant public health-related sectors, including child mortality, malnutrition, and HIV, was released in 2017. The two main public health issues that needed to be addressed during the next ten years, according to Gates, were infectious and chronic diseases.

A $12 million grant towards a universal flu vaccination was announced by Gates and Google co-founder Larry Page in April 2018. For individual initiatives that are "bold and innovative," he said the money would be given out in grants of up to $2 million, with the goal of starting clinical trials by 2021. While some questioned whether $12 million would be enough to spur any significant medical advancement, others welcomed the investment's goals, and Bill Gates suggested that there may be more to come.

Awards

Gates has won various honors for his charitable endeavors. Gates was listed as one of the most influential individuals of the 20th century by Time magazine. Along with Bono, the lead singer of the rock band U2, the magazine also picked Bill and Melinda Gates as its 2005 Persons of the Year.

Gates has received multiple honorary doctorates from international colleges. In 2005, Queen Elizabeth II conferred upon him the honorary knighthood of Knight Commander of the Order of the British Empire.

The Mexican government honored Gates and his wife with the Order of the Aztec

Eagle in 2006 for their global charitable efforts in the fields of health and education.

The pair received more recognition for their charitable endeavors in 2016 when President Barack Obama announced them as winners of the Presidential Medal of Freedom.

STEVE JOBS

Steve Jobs: Who Was He?

Steven Paul Jobs was an American inventor, designer and entrepreneur who was the co-founder, chief executive and chairman of Apple Computer. The iPod, iPhone, and iPad are just a few of Apple's ground-breaking inventions that have changed the course of contemporary technology.

Jobs, who was born in 1955 to two University of Wisconsin graduate students who put him up for adoption, was intelligent but aimless. He dropped out of school and tried his hand at a variety of activities before partnering with Steve Wozniak to co-found Apple in 1976. Jobs launched Pixar

Animation Studios after leaving the firm in 1985, and he eventually joined Apple more than ten years later. Jobs passed away in 2011 after a protracted fight with pancreatic cancer.

Parents of Steve Jobs and Adoption

Joanne Schieble (later Joanne Simpson) and Abdulfattah "John" Jandali, two PhD students at the University of Wisconsin, were the parents of Jobs. The parents placed their kid, who was nameless, for adoption.

Jandali Jobs, Jobs' father, was a professor of political science in Syria. Schieble, his mother, was a speech therapist. Shortly after Jobs was put for adoption, his birth parents married and had another child, Mona Simpson. Jobs wasn't able to learn more about his biological parents until he was 27 years old.

Jobs was given to Clara and Paul Jobs as a newborn, and was given the name Steven Paul Jobs. Clara worked as an accountant and Paul was a Coast Guard veteran and machinist.

Early Years

Jobs was born in San Francisco, California, on February 24, 1955. He resided in Mountain View, California, a region that would eventually come to be known as Silicon Valley, with his adopted family.

Jobs and his father worked on electronics in the garage when Jobs was a young lad. Paul taught his son how to disassemble and reassemble circuits; this activity gave the young Steve Jobs self-assurance, persistence, and mechanical skill.

Steve Jobs and Steve Wozniak

Jobs met Wozniak, his future business partner and co-founder of Apple Computer, while they were both students at Homestead High School back when Berkeley was Jobs' alma mater.

Wozniak explained why he and Jobs got along so well in a 2007 interview with PC World: "We both enjoyed technology and the way we used to wire together digital chips," he remarked. "At the time, almost anybody knew what chips were, how they operated, or what they were capable of. We shared interests even though I had created numerous computers and was much ahead of him in terms of electronics and computer design. We each had a largely distinct perspective on how the world worked.

Creating and Dismantling Apple Computer

In the Jobs family garage, at the age of barely 21, Jobs and Wozniak founded Apple Computer. Jobs sold his Volkswagen vehicle, and Wozniak sold his prized scientific calculator, to support their business endeavor. For Apple, Jobs and Wozniak are credited with democratizing technology, making devices smaller, less expensive, user-friendly, and available to regular people.

A line of user-friendly personal computers were created by Wozniak, and with Jobs in charge of marketing, Apple first sold them for $666.66 apiece. The Apple I brought in around $774,000 for the company. Sales for Apple soared by 700% to $139 million three years after the launch of the company's second product, the Apple II.

In 1980, Apple Computer went public and, at the conclusion of its first trading day, had a market value of $1.2 billion. To fill the position of Apple CEO, Jobs turned to Pepsi-Cola marketing guru John Sculley.

But Apple's subsequent products all had serious design problems, which led to recalls and unhappy customers. Sales of IBM abruptly overtook those of Apple, forcing Apple to contend with a business environment dominated by IBM/PCs.

Apple introduced the Macintosh in 1984 and promoted it as a component of a passionate, young, and creative counterculture lifestyle. Although the Macintosh had good sales and performed better than IBM's PCs, it was still not an IBM compatible product.

The leaders of the firm started to phase out Jobs because Sculley thought he was harming Apple. Jobs was forced into a more marginalized role at the firm he co-founded and departed in 1985 while not having an official title with it.

Next

Jobs founded NeXT, Inc. as a new hardware and software company in 1985 after quitting Apple. In 1996, Apple paid $429 million to acquire the firm after it failed to market its customized operating system to the majority of Americans.

Remaking Apple

Jobs reclaimed his position as CEO of Apple in 1997. Jobs is credited for reviving the firm in the 1990s, just as he was responsible for Apple's success in the 1970s.

Jobs resurrected Apple with a new management group, modified stock options, and a self-imposed yearly pay cap of $1. Consumers were once again drawn in by Jobs' innovative goods (like the iMac), strong branding initiatives, and fashionable looks.

In the years that followed, Apple unveiled devices that would change the face of technology, including the Macbook Air, iPod, and iPhone. The moment Apple unveiled a new device, other companies rushed to develop similar technology. In 2007, Apple's quarterly reports considerably improved: Shares were trading at a record-breaking $199.99 per share, the business had a remarkable $1.58 billion profit, a $18 billion cash surplus, and no debt.

Apple overtook Walmart as the second-largest music retailer in America in 2008, thanks to the success of its iTunes and iPod products. Apple has also been named first among Fortune 500 businesses for returns to shareholders and first on Fortune magazine's list of "America's Most Admired Companies."

Pixar and Steve Jobs

George Lucas sold Jobs an animation business in 1986, and that business subsequently evolved into Pixar Animation Studios. Jobs first put $50 million of his personal money into Pixar because he was confident in the company's potential.

The company went on to create hugely successful pictures including Toy Story, Finding Nemo, and The Incredibles; all of Pixar's productions have made $4 billion. Walt Disney and the studio combined in 2006, becoming Jobs Disney's biggest shareholder.

The bulk of Jobs' net wealth, according to a 2011 Forbes estimate, was between $6.5 billion and $7 billion as a result of his 2006 sale of Pixar to the Walt Disney Company. However, Jobs' net worth would have been an astounding $36 billion had he not sold his Apple shares in 1985, the year he left the organization he established and oversaw for nearly ten years.

Family

On March 18, 1991, Jobs and Laurene Powell were hitched. Powell was an MBA student at Stanford Business School when the two first crossed paths. Along with their three children, Reed, Erin, and Eve, they shared a home in Palo Alto, California.

In 1978, while he was 23 years old and dating Chrisann Brennan, Jobs also gave birth to a daughter named Lisa. In court records, he claimed he wasn't the father of his daughter and that he was infertile.

In her 2018 book Small Fry, Lisa Brennan Jobs writes about her youth and friendship with Jobs. According to Lisa, DNA testing showed that she and Jobs were a match in 1980, at which point he had to start paying child support to her mother, who was trying to make ends meet. Till she was 7 years old, Jobs did not approach his daughter about a relationship. Lisa moved in with her father when she was a teenager.

Fight against cancer

Jobs was diagnosed with a neuroendocrine tumor, an uncommon but treatable type of pancreatic cancer, in 2003. Jobs considered Eastern medical alternatives before delaying surgery and changing his pesco-vegetarian diet.

Jobs delayed surgery for nine months, alarmed Apple's board of directors. If news spread that their CEO was unwell, executives worried that investors would sell their shares. However, Jobs' privacy ultimately prevailed over shareholder disclosure.

Jobs had a successful procedure to remove the pancreatic tumor in 2004. True to pattern, Jobs said little little about his health in the years that followed.

Early in 2009, rumors concerning Jobs' weight loss spread, with some speculating that his health problems—which included a liver transplant—had reappeared. In response to these worries, Jobs said he was experiencing a hormonal imbalance. He took a six-month leave of absence a few days later.

Jobs referred to Tim Cook, Apple's chief operating officer, as "responsible for Apple's day-to-day operations" in an email to staff members after saying his "health-related concerns are more complicated" than he first imagined.

On September 9, 2009, Jobs gave a keynote speech at a private Apple event after almost a year away from the limelight. For the most of 2010, he continued to act as master of ceremonies, which included the iPad's introduction.

Jobs made the announcement about his medical leave in January 2011. He gave Cook the keys when he stepped down as Apple's CEO in August.

On October 5, 2011, Jobs passed away in Palo Alto after a nearly ten-year battle with pancreatic cancer. Age-wise, he was 56.

ELON MUSK

Elon Musk: Who Is He?

American entrepreneur and businessman Elon Musk, who was born in South Africa, created X.com in 1999 (which eventually evolved into PayPal), SpaceX in 2002, and Tesla Motors in 2003. When Musk sold his start-up firm, Zip2, to a subsidiary of Compaq Computers in his late 20s, he became a multimillionaire.

When SpaceX launched a rocket in May 2012 to deliver the first commercial vehicle to the International Space Station, Musk made headlines. By adding SolarCity to his portfolio in 2016 and accepting an advising position in the early months of President

Donald Trump's administration, he solidified his position as an industry leader.

According to reports, Musk will overtake Jeff Bezos as the richest person in the world in January 2021.

Early Years

Musk was born in Pretoria, South Africa, on June 28, 1971. When Musk was younger, his parents and physicians demanded a hearing test because he was so engrossed in his invention-related daydreams.

When Musk was 10 years old, just around the time of his parents' divorce, he started to get interested in computers. He learned how to write on his own, and at the age of 12, he sold his first piece of software—a game he had made named Blastar.

Musk was a scholarly, withdrawn, and short student in elementary school. He went through a growth spurt, was tormented until he was 15 years old, and learnt karate and wrestling as self-defense techniques.

Family

Maye Musk, Musk's mother, is a Canadian model and the oldest person to appear in a Covergirl advertisement. She once held five jobs at once to support her family when Musk was growing up.

Errol Musk, Musk's father, is a successful South African engineer.

With his sister Tosca and brother Kimbal, Musk spent his early years in South Africa. When he was 10 years old, his parents separated.

Individual Life

Two times, Musk has been married. In 2000, he married Justine Wilson, and the two went on to have six kids together. Their first child passed away from sudden infant death syndrome in 2002 at the age of 10 weeks (SIDS). Griffin and Xavier, twins, and Kai, Saxon, and Damian, triplets, were born in 2004. Musk and Wilson have had five further kids together (born in 2006).

Wilson and Musk had a rocky divorce before Musk met Talulah Riley. In 2010, the pair were hitched. After divorcing in 2012, they remarried in 2013. In the end, their marriage ended in divorce in 2016.

Girlfriends

Musk allegedly started dating actress Amber Heard in 2016, after the finalization of both their divorces from Johnny Depp and Riley. The pair parted in August 2017 due to their hectic schedules; they reconciled in January 2018 before breaking up once again a month later.

Musk started dating artist Grimes in May 2018. (born Claire Boucher). In the same month, Grimes said that she had changed her name to the letter "c," which stands for the speed of light, allegedly with Musk's support. Fans of the feminist musician attacked her for dating a millionaire whose business was dubbed a "predator zone" after allegations of sexual harassment.

In a March 2019 profile in the Wall Street Journal Magazine, the pair spoke about their love, with Grimes stating, "Look, I adore him, he's fantastic...

He's a damned intriguing individual, that's for sure. "I admire c's crazy fairy creative inventiveness and hyper-intense work ethic," Musk said in response to the Journal.

On May 4, 2020, Grimes gave birth to their baby, who they called "X A-12," as Musk announced. The couple said they were renaming their kid "X A-Xii" later in the month when it was reported that the State of California wouldn't allow a name containing a number.

Exa Dark Sideræl Musk, the couple's second child, was born to them in December 2021. The infant was born through a surrogate.

Education

Musk left South Africa at the age of 17 in 1989 to attend Queen's University and escape serving in the South African military's conscription program. In part because he believed it would be simpler to get American citizenship via that route, Musk became a citizen of Canada that year.

Musk left Canada in 1992 to attend the University of Pennsylvania to study physics and business. He earned an economics undergraduate degree before staying on to get a second bachelor's in physics.

Musk moved to Stanford University in California to seek a PhD in energy physics after leaving Penn. He left Stanford after only two days to join the Internet boom, starting his first firm, Zip2 Corporation, in 1995. However, his decision was made at the exact right moment. In 2002, Musk acceded to citizenship.

COMPANIES

Corporation Zip2

In 1995, Musk and his brother Kimbal Musk founded their first business, Zip2 Corporation. Zip2, an online city guide, quickly started contributing information to The New York Times and Chicago Tribune's new websites. For $307 million in cash and $34 million in stock options, a subsidiary of Compaq Computer Corporation acquired Zip2 in 1999.

PayPal

Elon and Kimbal Musk founded the online financial services and payments firm X.com in 1999 using the proceeds from the sale of Zip2. The next year, X.com was acquired, which resulted in the birth of PayPal as we know it today.

When PayPal was purchased by eBay for $1.5 billion in shares in October 2002, Musk made his first billion dollars. Musk controlled 11% of PayPal equity before the deal.

SpaceX

Space Exploration Technologies Corporation, or SpaceX, was formed by Musk in 2002 with the goal of developing spaceships for private space travel. In an effort to replace NASA's own space shuttle flights, NASA gave SpaceX a contract in 2008 to handle cargo transport for the

International Space Station, with intentions to include crew transport in the future.

Rockets the Falcon 9

Musk and SpaceX created history on May 22, 2012 when they sent an unmanned capsule into space on a Falcon 9 rocket. It was the first time a commercial firm has flown a spacecraft to the International Space Station, and it carried 1,000 pounds of supplies for the astronauts who were stationed there. Musk was reported as stating after the launch, "I feel really fortunate. It's comparable to winning the Super Bowl for us."

An orbital distance at which a satellite would lock into an orbital path that matched the rotation of the Earth was reached by a Falcon 9 rocket in December 2013 with success. A second Falcon 9 rocket carrying the Deep Space Climate Observatory (DSCOVR) satellite was launched by SpaceX in February 2015 with the purpose of observing the severe solar emissions that have an impact on the Earth's electrical networks and communications infrastructure.

A reusable-parts-built Falcon 9 rocket successfully test-flew and landed in March 2017 at SpaceX, ushering in a new era of more reasonably priced space travel.

An explosion that happened in November 2017 when the firm was testing its new Block 5 Merlin engine was a setback. No one was wounded, according to a statement from SpaceX, and the problem won't prevent the company from launching a new generation of Falcon 9 rockets as scheduled.

With the successful test launch of the powerful Falcon Heavy rocket in February 2018, the business celebrated yet another significant event. The Falcon Heavy was designed to lift massive payloads into orbit and perhaps act as a spacecraft for long space missions. It is equipped with multiple Falcon 9 rockets. Musk's cherry-red Tesla Roadster, which had cameras to "offer some amazing vistas" for the spacecraft's intended orbit around the sun, was loaded onto the Falcon Heavy for the test flight.

A new Block 5 Falcon rocket successfully landed on a drone ship in July 2018 for Space X less than nine minutes after takeoff.

Mars BFR Mission

In September 2017, Musk unveiled a new concept for his BFR, a 31-engine monster topped by a spacecraft designed to accommodate at least 100 people. BFR is an abbreviation for either "Big F—-ing Rocket" or "Big Falcon Rocket." As part of his overall plan to colonize the Red Planet, Elon said that SpaceX intended to fly the first cargo flights to Mars with the craft in 2022.

The businessman gave a knowing gesture to his prior issues with meeting timelines when he said, in March 2018, to an audience at the annual South by Southwest festival in Austin, Texas, that he intended to have the BFR ready for brief flights early the following year.

It was revealed the following month that SpaceX will establish a facility in the Port of Los Angeles to create and host the BFR. SpaceX found the port property to be the perfect site since, once finished, its enormous rocket can only be moved by barge or ship.

Internet satellites from Starlink

The U.S. government gave SpaceX approval to launch a fleet of satellites into low orbit for the purpose of delivering Internet connectivity in late March 2018. The Starlink satellite network aims to increase competition in densely populated markets that are now controlled by one or two providers while simultaneously improving broadband service accessibility in remote regions.

In May 2019, SpaceX launched the first batch of 60 satellites, then in November of the same year, it launched a second payload of 60 satellites. Although this was a significant step forward for the Starlink project, the appearance of these bright orbiters in the night sky, with the possibility of thousands more to follow, alarmed astronomers who believed that the proliferation of satellites would make it more challenging to observe far-off objects in space.

THE TESLA MOTORS

Musk is a co-founder, CEO, and product architect of Tesla Motors, a business founded in 2003 with a focus on mass-market, reasonably priced electric vehicles as well as battery goods and solar roofs. Musk is in charge of all aspects of product development, engineering, and design for the business.

Roadster

Five years after the company's founding, in March 2008, Tesla launched the Roadster, a sports vehicle with a lithium ion battery that allows it to go almost 250 miles between charges and accelerate from 0 to 60 mph in under 3.7 seconds.

Tesla Motors announced its first public offering in June 2010, generating $226 million thanks to a stake Daimler had purchased in the business and a strategic alliance with Toyota.

Design S

The Model S, Tesla's first electric sedan that was apparently intended to compete with the BMW 5 series, was originally introduced in August 2008. The Model S started out in production in 2012 with a starting price of $58,570. It was recognized by Motor Trend magazine as the 2013 Car of the Year because to its 265-mile range between charges.

Tesla declared in April 2017 that it has overtaken General Motors to become the most valued American automaker. Tesla, which planned to increase production and introduce its Model 3 vehicle later that year, benefited greatly from the news.

At Laguna Seca Raceway in Monterey County, California, in September 2019, a Model S achieved a speed record for a four-door sedan utilizing what Musk referred to as a "Plaid powertrain."

Model 3

Early in 2019, the Model 3 was finally introduced after lengthy manufacturing delays. The car's starting price of $35,000 made it far more affordable than Tesla's Model S and X electric cars, which start at $69,500 and go higher from there.

Musk had originally planned to create 5,000 brand-new Model 3 vehicles per week by the end of 2017, but he later shifted that target out to March 2018 and then to June when the new year began. Industry analysts were not surprised by the stated delay since they were aware of the company's manufacturing issues; nonetheless, some questioned how long investors would be willing to wait. It also didn't stop Musk from obtaining an innovative new remuneration arrangement as CEO, in which he would be rewarded upon the achievement of increasing value goals based on $50 billion increments.

By April 2018, it was reported that Musk had fired the engineering division's director in order to personally direct efforts there since Tesla was anticipated to fall short of first-quarter production estimates. Musk remarked in a Twitter conversation with a reporter that it was crucial to "divide and conquer" in order to achieve production targets and that he was "back to sleeping at the plant."

Musk hinted that the firm might restructure its management structure before announcing in June that Tesla was firing 9% of its workers while keeping its manufacturing division intact. Musk acknowledged that it was time to start making real efforts toward generating a profit in an email to staff, explaining his intention to remove some "duplicate of responsibilities" in order to save expenses. Tesla said that it had achieved its objective of manufacturing 5,000 Model 3 vehicles per week by the end of June 2018 while also generating an additional 2,000 Model S sedans and Model X SUVs, indicating that the reorganization had paid off. Musk exclaimed, "We did it!" in a joyful email to the business. What a fantastic work, done by a fantastic crew.

Musk said that the business was finally releasing its regular Model 3 in February of the following year. Musk also said that Tesla was switching to entirely online sales and giving buyers the option to return their vehicles for a full refund within seven days or 1,000 miles.

Large Truck

When the new Tesla Semi and Roadster were unveiled at the company's design studio in November 2017, Musk made another impact. The semi-truck claims a 500-mile range, a battery and motors designed to last a million miles, and was originally scheduled to go into production in 2019 before being postponed.

Roadster and Model Y

Musk introduced Tesla's much anticipated Model Y in March 2019. The 300-mile driving range and 3.5-second 0 to 60 mph pace of the tiny crossover, which started shipping to consumers in March 2020.

With a 0 to 60 duration of 1.9 seconds, the 2020 Roadster will surpass all other production vehicles in terms of speed.

SolarCity

In August 2016, a $2.6 billion agreement was finalized to unite Musk's electric vehicle and solar energy businesses. This was part of Musk's ongoing efforts to create sustainable energy and goods for a larger customer base. In an all-stock agreement, Musk's Tesla Motors Inc. purchased

SolarCity Corp., a business his cousins and he co-founded in 2006. He has the bulk of the stock in each company.

"When used together, solar and storage perform optimally. A statement on Tesla's website regarding the partnership said, "As one business, Tesla (storage) and SolarCity (solar) can develop fully integrated residential, commercial, and grid-scale solutions that enhance the way energy is produced, stored, and consumed.

The Dull Company

Musk established The Boring Company in January 2017, a business focused to drilling and constructing tunnels to lessen traffic on the streets. On the SpaceX facility near Los Angeles, he started by digging a test hole.

Musk published the first image of his company's development on his Instagram feed in late October of that year. He said that it would take about four months for the 500-foot tunnel, which would typically run parallel to Interstate 405, to reach a length of two miles.

The Las Vegas Convention and Visitors Authority awarded the business, now known as TBC, a $48.7 million contract in May 2019 for the construction of an underground Loop system to transport visitors around the Las Vegas Convention Center.

Musk's Tweet and the SEC's inquiry

In a tweet on August 7, 2018, Musk revealed a shocking revelation: "At $420, I'm thinking about taking Tesla private. funding arranged." Due to the SEC's inquiries into whether Musk had really obtained the funds as reported, the revelation made the firm and its creator vulnerable to legal action. According to many lawsuits brought by investors, Musk's tweet was intended to ambush short sellers and influence stock prices.

Tesla stock originally spiked in response to Musk's statement, but it eventually finished the day up 11%. In a message published as a follow-up on the business blog, the CEO referred to the decision to go private as "the best road ahead." He pledged to keep his investment in the business and stated that he would establish a special fund to support the continued participation of all present investors.

Six days later, Musk released a statement to explain his stance. In it, he cited his "funding secured" claim as the result of conversations with the managing director of the Saudi Arabian sovereign wealth fund. Later, he tweeted that he was developing a plan to take Tesla private with the help of Goldman Sachs and Silver Lake as financial consultants.

That day, rapper Azealia Banks said on Instagram that when she was a visitor at Elon Musk's house at the time, she discovered that he was under the influence of LSD when he sent out his news-grabbing tweet. Banks claimed to have overheard Musk on the phone trying to get the cash he had said was already in place.

When it was revealed that two legal firms had been hired by Tesla's outside board to handle the SEC investigation and the CEO's ambitions to take the business private, the story soon took on a serious tone once again.

Musk said on August 24 that he had changed his mind and would not be taking the firm private, a day after meeting with the board. He listed the wish of the majority of directors to keep Tesla publicly traded as one of his justifications, along with the challenge of maintaining some of the major shareholders who were precluded from engaging in a private business. Others said that Musk was also affected by the unfavorable perception of an electric vehicle firm receiving funding from Saudi Arabia, a nation with a significant oil sector presence.

As part of a settlement with the SEC, Musk was required to pay a $20 million fine and vacate his position as Tesla's board chairman for a period of three years, it was revealed on September 29, 2018.

INVENTIONS AND INNOVATIONS

Hyperloop

In August 2013, Musk released a concept for a new form of transportation called the "Hyperloop," an invention that would foster commuting between major cities while severely cutting travel time. Ideally resistant to weather and powered by renewable energy, the Hyperloop would propel riders in pods through a network of low-pressure tubes at speeds reaching more than 700 mph. Musk noted that the Hyperloop could take from seven to 10 years to be built and ready for use.

Although he introduced the Hyperloop with claims that it would be safer than a plane or train, with an estimated cost of $6 billion — approximately one-tenth of the cost for the rail system planned by the state of California — Musk's concept has drawn skepticism. Nevertheless, the entrepreneur has sought to encourage the development of this idea.

After he announced a competition for teams to submit their designs for a Hyperloop pod prototype, the first Hyperloop Pod Competition was held at the SpaceX facility in January 2017. A speed record of 284 mph was set by a German student engineering team at competition No. 3 in 2018, with the same team pushing the record to 287 mph the next year.

AI and Neuralink

Musk has pursued an interest in artificial intelligence, becoming co-chair of the nonprofit OpenAI. The research company launched in late 2015 with the stated mission of advancing digital intelligence to benefit humanity.

In 2017, it was also reported that Musk was backing a venture called Neuralink, which intends to create devices to be implanted in the human brain and help people merge with software. He expanded on the company's progress during a July 2019 discussion, revealing that its devices will consist of a microscopic chip that connects via Bluetooth to a smartphone.

High-Speed Train

In late November 2017, after Chicago Mayor Rahm Emanuel asked for proposals to build and operate a high-speed rail line that would transport passengers from O'Hare Airport to downtown Chicago in 20 minutes or less, Musk tweeted that he was all-in on the competition with The Boring Company. He said that the concept of the Chicago loop would be different from his Hyperloop, its relatively short route not requiring the need for drawing a vacuum to eliminate air friction.

In summer 2018 Musk announced he would cover the estimated $1 billion needed to dig the 17-mile tunnel from the airport to downtown Chicago. However, in late 2019 he tweeted that TBC would focus on completing the commercial tunnel in Las Vegas before turning to other projects, suggesting that plans for Chicago would remain in limbo for the immediate future.

Flamethrower

Musk also reportedly found a market for The Boring Company's flamethrowers. After announcing they were going on sale for $500 apiece in late January 2018, he claimed to have sold 10,000 of them within a day.

Relationship with Donald Trump

In December 2016, Musk was named to President Trump's Strategy and Policy Forum; the following January, he joined Trump's Manufacturing Jobs Initiative. Following Trump's election, Musk found himself on common ground with the new president and his advisers as the president announced plans to pursue massive infrastructure developments.

While sometimes at odds with the president's controversial measures, such as a proposed ban on immigrants from Muslim-majority countries, Musk defended his involvement with the new administration. "My goals," he tweeted in early 2017, "are to accelerate the world's transition to sustainable energy and to help make humanity a multi-planet civilization, a consequence of which will be the creating of hundreds of thousands of jobs and a more inspiring future for all."

On June 1, following Trump's announcement that he was withdrawing the U.S. from the Paris climate accord, Musk stepped down from his advisory roles.

Volunteer Work

Musk established the Musk Foundation, which is committed to space exploration and the search for renewable and sustainable energy sources, in order to further his long-standing interests in the limitless potential of space exploration and the protection of the future of the human race.

Musk said in October 2019 that he will give $1 million to the #TeamTrees initiative, which seeks to plant 20 million trees worldwide by the year 2020. For the occasion, he even changed his Twitter handle to Treelon.

9 HABITS OF HIGHLY EFFECTIVE AND SUCCESSFUL PEOPLE.

1. Wealthy individuals are conservative spenders

Mark Zuckerberg, the founder of Facebook, is renowned for arriving to work in unadorned t-shirts. Bill Gates seldom appears in a well-fitted suit. Checking your spending habits is the best approach to get wealthy one day. This is evident in people's appearance and manner of life. Only the necessities are purchased by the wealthy.

2. Rather than overcrowding their houses with possessions, they prioritize increasing their money.

That explains why some of the world's wealthiest individuals don't lead showy lives. Rich people don't try to seem wealthy. They are aware of this (or will get there).

3. They invest instead of saving.

Traditional saving is not a term that the wealthy use. They don't deposit their spare cash in banks or other institutions. The wealthy are always looking for methods to invest their amassed wealth and get returns greater than those offered by traditional institutions.

The folks who truly pay attention to what experts say—that money sitting in banks loses value over time—are the ones who succeed in life. Cash is worthless due to inflation unless it is yielding returns that are greater than its yearly rate. The wealthiest individuals in the world either have their money invested in businesses, common stocks, or real estate, all of which experience inflation rates higher than those of the macroeconomy. They earn money by using it.

4. Their acquaintance is debt

Robert Kiyosaki used real estate to create his fortune. He would get bank loans to finance homes, then rent them out to pay the EMIs. Formerly the wealthiest man in Asia, Mukesh Ambani owes his firm, Reliance Industries Limited, a total of INR 2.87 lakh crore in debt. Rich people lend money or incur debts to their pals. They increase their riches by taking advantage of the yearly payouts. They never allow their debt to balloon and force them into bankruptcy. Simply stated, they understand how to employ fast personal loans and short-term loans to grow their company.

5. *They seldom ever wager their whole bankroll.*

The first rule of being wealthy, according to seasoned investor and one of the top five wealthiest men in the world, Warren Buffett, is to never lose money. Gambling does not appear in his books since he thinks that the best investments are those that are guaranteed to provide profits. Unscrupulous investments undervalue collected funds, and those who try to gamble their way to wealth nearly invariably fail. Similar concepts apply when playing poker or purchasing lottery tickets, when the odds of success are slim.

6. *Rely on systematic investment strategies*

Large market fluctuations are seen on every financial channel. They increase during economic booms and decrease during downturns. Nobody is able to correctly forecast when or how the market will act. Rich people use systematic investment plans, or SIPs, to their benefit until they have accumulated enough expertise to make forecasts. While you pay a certain amount each month, you may purchase more when interest rates are low and invest less when they rise. The total return is favorable, and it enables you to gradually increase your money. Any wealthy person you ask will tell you how they were able to capitalize on the power of planned investment.

7. They consider the long term.

The wealthy do not invest their money in short-term projects, whether they be SIPs, stocks, properties, or private investments. They think in terms of decades rather than weeks or a few years. Tesla was formed by Elon Musk back in 2003, but it wasn't until lately that the business achieved stock market success and allowed Musk to enter the exclusive group of the super-rich. Wealth accumulation is a long-term endeavor. The wealthy stay away from short-term investments because they gobble up earnings in brokerage and taxes.

8. They prioritize passion above money.

Elon Musk is perhaps the best illustration of how a person's passion can lead to financial success. His early desire was to create secure automobiles, and Tesla is the realization of that dream. The business had been losing money for years until its share price shot beyond $700 in February 2020. Additionally, Robert Kiyosaki said in an interview that he keeps making real estate investments because he enjoys doing so. And it was Jeff Bezos' love of reading that inspired him to start Amazon. The wealthy continue to follow their passions because they know that the secret to perseverance is to first enjoy something before finding a way to profit from it.

9. They possess patience.

Market fluctuations don't concern them. They are aware that everything happens, happens for a reason. This is the reason Warren Buffett owns a 23% interest in Apple Inc., despite the fact that the company's value has declined since its high. The wealthy let their investments and fortune be determined by their patience. They let their choices weather the rough patch and flourish once the sun comes out again. According to Buffett, money in the stock market moves from the active to the patient, and the latter reaps the greatest rewards by being quiet.

8 THINGS TO TAKE AWAY FROM THESE MEN

1. Rich individuals don't first want riches.

Instead, they follow a passion. Henry Ford followed his quest for a vehicle without horses. Steve Jobs, Warren Buffett, and Bill Gates all followed their inclinations. The thing about passion is that it propels individuals to advance, to keep pushing ahead, and to resist giving in to failure or despair. The rest of us work to make money.

We choose careers that will pay enough for us to live comfortably; we get increases and promotions, and our standard of living rises. As we earn more money, we spend more, which leads us to seek out more money to spend. Contrarily, the affluent developed a love for something early on—investing, driving, or computer technology—and they were prepared to go hungry so they could follow that drive.

2. *Rich folks relish their discomfort.*

The rest of us just want to feel at ease. Uncertainty drives wealthy individuals, and they like taking chances when they are unsure of the results. Ordinary people often avoid taking significant risks and dislike being uncomfortable. Throughout our history, self-made millionaires have shown a willingness to take significant risks.

3. *Even though the future may be unknown, wealthy individuals are optimistic about what lies ahead.*

The "better" life is often seen by the average person as having been lived in the past.

People weren't glued to their electronics, life was easier, and genuine men really went out and made a solid livelihood for their families. The music was also better back then. These individuals have a pessimistic outlook on the future and often assert that everything's just "falling apart." People grow stagnant and lack huge goals when they don't aim toward a better future. Wealthy individuals are more likely to feel upbeat and take action to build a better future.

4. People that are wealthy have a big plan.

Ordinary people have plans and aspirations for their future selves, their children, and even how they want to spend their retirement years. But the wealthy have great goals that have nothing to do with their personal life. They have ideas that will significantly alter things. With their Big Plan, they want to improve the planet.

5. Rich individuals maintain their confidence.

They have gained this confidence in a variety of ways, failure being only one of them. They make mistakes, learn from them, and move on. They practice confidence because they are aware of how important it is in the "fight" for money.

When they go beyond their comfort zones, average individuals lack confidence, and failure may harm or even destroy their self-assurance. Wealthy individuals gain confidence when they achieve success. Success for average individuals leads to better employment and more money, but none of these factors boosts confidence. Their self-confidence grows as a result of taking chances and eventually succeeding despite several setbacks. They eventually adopt the mentality that there is nothing they cannot do. "Whether you believe that you can or you can't, you are typically correct," stated Henry Ford, summarizing the situation.

6. Rich individuals are selective in their friendships.

Old friends and distant relatives will start to show up in the life of the wealthy once they become wealthy. Their objectives are rather obvious: they want a share of the money that has been collected. They get hostile when their pleas for loans and/or money are rejected. "You witness a terrible part of our human life, which is the world of false pretenses demanding your money," said Fisher Investments' billionaire owner Ken Fisher.

7. *Wealthy individuals are aware that discipline is necessary to build wealth.*

This is particularly true during the time of accumulation. They do not possess brand-new automobiles or the greatest homes that their salary may permit, they live below their means, and they dress modestly. They are aware that in order to become affluent, they must invest and save money while pursuing their hobbies. Because they want or need to impress others with what they can afford to buy, regular people want to acquire items as soon as their money allows them to. They don't invest or save money; instead, they depend on social security and retirement funds to maintain their standard of living in old age.

8. People with money don't worry about failing.

They are aware that they could fail and that investing all of their money might result in financial loss. They are also aware that their next business endeavor may be the one that both fulfills their passion and brings them financial success. The majority of individuals are afraid to fail. They worry about not having enough money and about losing their job's reliable source of income. People who always live in terror will never become wealthy. However, they are most afraid of failing since it would result in all the other things they are afraid of.

www.ingramcontent.com/pod-product-compliance
Lightning Source LLC
Chambersburg PA
CBHW070239220526
45465CB00004B/1457